HISTORY'S MOST INFLUENTIAL

PHILOSOPHERS

FROM THE Late 1800s TO THE Mid-1900s

Gottlob Frege to Jean-Paul Sartre

EDITED BY BRIAN DUIGNAN

Britannica® Educational Publishing
IN ASSOCIATION WITH
ROSEN
EDUCATIONAL SERVICES

Published in 2025 by Britannica Educational Publishing
(a trademark of Encyclopædia Britannica, Inc.)
in association with Rosen Educational Services, LLC
2544 Clinton Street, Buffalo, NY 14224.

Distributed exclusively by Rosen Educational Services.
For a listing of additional Britannica Educational Publishing titles, call toll free (800) 237-9932.

First Edition

Britannica Educational Publishing
Michael I. Levy: Executive Editor
Marilyn L. Barton: Senior Coordinator, Production Control
Steven Bosco: Director, Editorial Technologies
Lisa S. Braucher: Senior Producer and Data Editor
Yvette Charboneau: Senior Copy Editor
Kathy Nakamura: Manager, Media Acquisition
Robert Curley: Manager, Science and Technology

Editor: Greg Roza
Book design: Michael Flynn

Photo credits: Cover https://commons.wikimedia.org/wiki/File:Martin_Buber_1963.jpg; p. 41 https://commons.wikimedia.org/wiki/File:Ludwig_Wittgenstein.jpg.

Cataloging-in-Publication Data

Names: Duignan, Brian.
Title: From the late 1800s to the mid-1900s: Gottlob Frege to Jean-Paul Sartre / edited by Brian Duignan.
Description: New York : Britannica Educational Publishing, in Association with Rosen Educational Services, 2025. | Series: History's most influential philosophers | Includes glossary and index.
Identifiers: ISBN 9781641904070 (library bound) | ISBN 9781641904063 (pbk) | ISBN 9781641904087 (ebook)
Subjects: LCSH: Philosophers--Biography. | Philosophy--History. | Philosophy. | Philosophers.
Classification: LCC B104.F766 2025 | DDC 109.2--dc23

Manufactured in the United States of America

CPSIA Compliance Information: Batch #CWBRIT25. For further information contact Rosen Publishing at 1-800-237-9932.

CONTENTS

INTRODUCTION

"The good life is one inspired by love and guided by knowledge."
—Bertrand Russell (1872–1970)

Life doesn't come with an instruction manual. Each person is left to find their own way to some sort of understanding about the mysteries of existence. As people grow and learn, they naturally ask questions. How did the world—and universe—come to exist? Why am I here? What is my purpose in life? What happens after I die?

People began their search for meaning very early on in the course of human history. Long before the age of science, they used reason to understand why things happened as they did, and to find some sort of order and security in what they saw as a chaotic and often dangerous world. They questioned, probed, and refused to accept commonly held beliefs. Through their teachings, the discipline of philosophy was born.

In the simplest terms, philosophy is about thinking. Yet philosophers do a lot more than sit around thinking and asking questions. They engage in fundamental discussions about nature, society, science, psychology, and ethics. They develop critical ideas about the way people live, and the way they should live. Traveling through the pages of this book, you will discover the events and the people that shaped philosophy from the late 1800s to the mid-1900s.

Three basic principles guide philosophical thought. The first is ontology, which is the study of existence—why we are here. Some philosophers have used philosophy to defend religion and contemplate the existence of God. Martin Buber was a Jewish philosopher from this period whose work focused on the dynamics of human relationships and ultimately examined relations between individuals and God. Other thinkers used philosophy to dispute religious beliefs. French Existentialist Jean-Paul Sartre denied the existence of any God or human soul. The only thing that truly exists, he said, is the way things appear to us, or our perception of things. In Sartre's view, all individuals have the freedom to assign their own meaning to life.

The second principle of philosophy, epistemology, involves the study of knowledge—how we know what we know. This leads to ideas about the origins of knowledge and how knowledge is obtained. Many of the philosophers profiled in this volume were concerned with questions of knowledge and logic. Friedrich Ludwig Gottlob Frege, Alfred North Whitehead, Bertrand Russell, and Ludwig Wittgenstein studied the relationship between mathematics, logic, and philosophy.

The final of the three guiding philosophical principles is ethics, or the study of what is right and wrong. The fundamental nature of humankind has long challenged the great philosophers. Are people born inherently good, evil, or somewhere in between? And how do people know which actions are good or evil, right or wrong? G. E. Moore became known as an "ethical intuitionist" for his idea that what is good is known through intuition and that common sense generally points toward truth.

The great thinkers whose lives and beliefs are detailed in these pages have helped give shape and depth to human existence. And yet philosophy is constantly evolving. Just as some questions are answered, new questions emerge. Expect the list of influential philosophers to grow over the years as people continue to probe and wonder about the great mysteries of the universe and human existence.

FRIEDRICH LUDWIG GOTTLOB FREGE

(b. Nov. 8, 1848, Wismar, Mecklenburg-Schwerin, Ger.—d. July 26, 1925, Bad Kleinen)

Gottlob Frege was a German philosopher, logician, and mathematician who founded modern mathematical logic. Frege discovered, on his own, the fundamental ideas that have made possible the whole modern development of logic and thereby invented an entire discipline.

Frege was the son of Alexander Frege, a principal of a girls' high school in Wismar. His mother, Auguste Frege, *née* Bialloblotzky, who was perhaps of Polish origin, outlived her husband, who died in 1866. Frege entered the University of Jena in 1869, where he studied for two years, and then went to the University of Göttingen for a further two—in mathematics, physics, chemistry, and philosophy. Frege spent the whole of his working life as a teacher of mathematics at Jena: he became a *Privatdozent* in May 1871, was made an *ausserordentlicher Professor* (associate professor) in July 1879, and became statutory professor of mathematics in May 1896.

Frege had a vivid awareness of his own genius and a belief that it would one day be recognized; but he became increasingly embittered at the failure of scholars to recognize it during his lifetime. He delighted in controversy and polemic; but the originality of his own work, the almost total independence of his own ideas from other influences, past or present, was quite exceptional and, indeed, astonishing.

System of Mathematical Logic

In 1879 Frege published his *Begriffsschrift* ("Conceptscript"), in which, for the first time, a system of mathematical logic in the modern sense was presented. There followed a period of intensive work on the philosophy of logic and of mathematics, embodied initially in his first book, *Die Grundlagen der Arithmetik* (1884; *The Foundations of Arithmetic*). Frege returned to the philosophy of mathematics with the first volume of *Grundgesetze der Arithmetik* (1893; partial Eng. trans., *Basic Laws of Arithmetic*), in which he presented, in a modified version of the symbolic system of the *Begriffsschrift*, a rigorous development of the theory of *Grundlagen*.

Contradictions in Frege's System

While volume 2 of the *Grundgesetze* was at the printer's, Frege received a letter from one of the few contemporaries who had read and admired his works—Bertrand Russell. The latter pointed out, modestly but correctly, the possibility of deriving a contradiction in Frege's logical system—the celebrated Russell paradox.

At this point Frege's productive life effectively ceased. He never published the projected third volume of the *Grundgesetze*, and he took no part in the development of the subject, mathematical logic, that he had founded, though it had progressed considerably by the time of his death. In 1912 he declined, in terms expressing deep depression, an invitation by Russell to address a mathematical congress in Cambridge.

Frege's system of mathematical logic frequently was not comprehended clearly when first presented. Some decades later, however, when the subject began to get under way, his ideas reached others mostly as filtered through the minds of other men, such as Peano. In his lifetime there were very few—one was Russell—to give Frege the credit due him.

EDMUND HUSSERL

(b. April 8, 1859, Prossnitz, Moravia, Austrian Empire [now Prostějov, Czech Republic]—d. April 27, 1938, Freiburg im Breisgau, Ger.)

Edmund Husserl was a German philosopher and the founder of phenomenology, a method for the description and analysis of consciousness through which philosophy attempts to gain the character of a strict science.

Husserl was born into a Jewish family and completed his qualifying examinations in 1876 at the German public gymnasium in the neighboring city of Olmütz (Olomouc). He then studied physics, mathematics, astronomy, and philosophy at the universities of Leipzig, Berlin, and Vienna. In Vienna he received his doctor of philosophy degree in 1882 with a dissertation entitled *Beiträge zur Theorie der Variationsrechnung* ("Contributions to the Theory of the Calculus of Variations").

In the autumn of 1883, Husserl moved to Vienna to study with the philosopher and psychologist Franz Brentano. In Vienna Husserl converted to the Evangelical Lutheran faith, and one year later, in 1887, he married Malvine Steinschneider, the daughter of a secondary-school professor from Prossnitz.

Lecturer at Halle

In 1886 Husserl went—with a recommendation from Brentano—to Carl Stumpf, the oldest of Brentano's students, who had further developed his psychology and who was professor of philosophy and psychology at the University of Halle. In 1887 Husserl qualified as a lecturer at the University of Halle with a *Habilitation* thesis—*Über den Begriff der Zahl: Psychologische Analysen* ("On the Concept of Number: Psychological Analyses")—that showed him in the transition from his mathematical research to a reflection upon the psychological source of the basic concepts of mathematics.

The years of his teaching in Halle (1887–1901) were later seen by Husserl to have been his most difficult. The problem of uniting a psychological analysis of consciousness with a philosophical grounding of formal mathematics and logic seemed insoluble. But from this crisis there emerged the insight that the philosophical grounding of logic and mathematics must commence with an analysis of the experience that lies before all formal thinking.

The fruits of this realization were presented in the *Logische Untersuchungen* (1900–01; "Logical Investigations"), which employed a method of analysis that Husserl now designated as "phenomenological." The revolutionary significance of this work was only gradually recognized, for its method could not be subsumed under any of the philosophical orientations well known at that time.

Phenomenology as the Universal Science

As a university lecturer at the University of Göttingen (1901–16) Husserl drafted the outline of phenomenology as a universal philosophical science. Its fundamental methodological principle was what Husserl called the phenomenological reduction. It focuses the philosopher's attention on uninterpreted basic experience and the quest, thereby, for the essences of things. In this sense, it is "eidetic" reduction. On the other hand, it is also the reflection on the functions by which essences become conscious. As such, the reduction reveals the ego for which everything has meaning. Hence, phenomenology took on the character of a new style of transcendental philosophy, which repeats and improves Kant's mediation between Empiricism and Rationalism in a modern way. Husserl presented its program and its systematic outline in the

Ideen zu einer reinen Phänomenologie und phänomenologischen Philosophie (1913; *Ideas; General Introduction to Pure Phenomenology*), of which, however, only the first part was completed.

The Renewal of Spiritual Life

His call in 1916 to the position of *ordentlicher Professor* (university professor) at the University of Freiburg meant a new beginning for Husserl in every respect. His inaugural lecture on "Die reine Phänomenologie, ihr Forschungsgebiet und ihre Methode" ("Pure Phenomenology, Its Area of Research and Its Method") circumscribed his program of work. He had understood World War I as the collapse of the old European world, in which spiritual culture, science, and philosophy had held an incontestable position. In this situation, the epistemological grounding that he had previously provided for phenomenology no longer satisfied him; after this, his reflections were directed with special emphasis upon philosophy's task in the renewal of life.

In this sense he had set forth in his lectures on *Erste Philosophie* (1923–24; "First Philosophy") the thesis that phenomenology, with its method of reduction, is the way to the absolute vindication of life—i.e., to the realization of the ethical autonomy of man. Upon this basis, he continued his clarification of the relation between a psychological and a phenomenological analysis of consciousness and his research into the grounding of logic, which he published as the *Formale und transzendentale Logik: Versuch einer Kritik der logischen Vernunft* (1929; *Formal and Transcendental Logic*, 1969).

When he retired in 1928, Martin Heidegger, who was destined to become a leading Existentialist and one of Germany's foremost philosophers, became his successor.

Husserl had looked upon him as his legitimate heir. Only later did he see that Heidegger's chief work, *Sein und Zeit* (1927; *Being and Time*, 1962), had given phenomenology a turn that would lead down an entirely different path. Husserl's disappointment led to a cooling of their relationship after 1930.

Later Years

Adolf Hitler's seizure of power in 1933 did not break Husserl's ability to work. Rather, the experience of this upheaval was, for him, the occasion for concentrating more than ever upon phenomenology's task of preserving the freedom of the mind. He was excluded from the university; but the loneliness of his study was broken through his daily philosophical walks with his research assistant, Eugen Fink, through his friendships with a few colleagues who belonged to the circles of the resistance and the "Denominational Church," and through numerous visits by foreign philosophers and scholars.

In the summer of 1937, the illness that made it impossible for him to continue his work set in. From the beginning of 1938 he saw only one remaining task: to be able to die in a way worthy of a philosopher. He died in April 1938, and his ashes were buried in the cemetery in Günterstal near Freiburg.

HENRI BERGSON

(b. Oct. 18, 1859, Paris, France—d. Jan. 4, 1941, Paris)

Henri Bergson, a French philosopher, was the first to elaborate what came to be called a process philosophy. He was awarded the Nobel Prize for Literature in 1927.

Through his father, a talented musician, Bergson was

descended from a rich Polish Jewish family. His mother came from an English Jewish family. Bergson's upbringing, training, and interests were typically French, and his professional career, as indeed all of his life, was spent in France, most of it in Paris.

Bergson received a doctorate in 1889 for his *Essai sur les données immédiates de la conscience* (*Time and Free Will: An Essay on the Immediate Data of Consciousness*). This work was primarily an attempt to establish the notion of duration, or lived time, as opposed to what he viewed as the spatialized conception of time, measured by a clock, that is employed by science. He proceeded by analyzing the awareness that man has of his inner self to show that psychological facts are qualitatively different from any other, charging psychologists in particular with falsifying the facts by trying to quantify and number them. Once the confusions were cleared away that confounded duration with extension, succession with simultaneity, and quality with quantity, he maintained that the objections to human liberty made in the name of scientific determinism could be seen to be baseless.

Philosophical Triumphs

The publication of the *Essai* found Bergson returned to Paris, teaching at the Lycée Henri IV. In 1891 he married Louise Neuburger, a cousin of the French novelist Marcel Proust. Meanwhile, he had undertaken the study of the relation between mind and body. Though he was convinced that he had refuted the argument for determinism, his own work, in the doctoral dissertation, had not attempted to explain how mind and body are related. The findings of his research into this problem were published in 1896 under the title *Matière et mémoire: essai sur la relation du corps à l'esprit* (*Matter and Memory*).

The *Essai* had been widely reviewed in the professional journals, but *Matière et mémoire* attracted the attention of a wider audience and marked the first step along the way that led to Bergson's becoming one of the most popular and influential lecturers and writers of the day. *L'Évolution créatrice* (1907; *Creative Evolution*), the greatest work of these years and Bergson's most famous book, reveals him most clearly as a philosopher of process at the same time that it shows the influence of biology upon his thought. In examining the idea of life, Bergson accepted evolution as a scientifically established fact. But he proposed that the whole evolutionary process should be seen as the endurance of an *élan vital* ("vital impulse") that is continually developing and generating new forms.

Later Years

In 1914 Bergson retired from all active duties at the Collège de France, although he did not formally retire from the chair until 1921. Having received the highest honors that France could offer him, including membership, since 1915, among the "40 immortals" of the Académie Française, he was awarded the Nobel Prize for Literature in 1927.

In 1932 he published *Les Deux Sources de la morale et de la religion* (*The Two Sources of Morality and Religion*). Here he came much closer to the orthodox religious notion of God than he had in the vital impulse of *L'Évolution créatrice*. He acknowledged in his will of 1937, "My reflections have led me closer and closer to Catholicism, in which I see the complete fulfillment of Judaism." Yet, although declaring his "moral adherence to Catholicism," he never went beyond that. In explanation, he wrote: "I would have become a convert, had I not foreseen for years a formidable wave of anti-Semitism about to break upon the world. I wanted to remain among those who tomorrow were to be persecuted." To confirm this conviction, only a few weeks before his death, he arose from his sickbed and stood in line in order to register as a Jew, in accord with the law just imposed by the Vichy government and from which he refused the exemption that had been offered him.

JOHN DEWEY

(b. Oct. 20, 1859, Burlington, Vt., U.S.—d. June 1, 1952, New York, N.Y.)

John Dewey, an American philosopher and educator, was one of the founders of the philosophical school of pragmatism, a pioneer in functional psychology, and a leader of the progressive movement in education in the United States.

The son of a grocer in Vermont, Dewey attended the public schools of Burlington and there entered the University of Vermont. After being awarded the PhD degree by Johns Hopkins University in 1884, Dewey, in the fall of that year, went to the University of Michigan, where he had been appointed an instructor in philosophy and psychology. With the exception of the academic year 1888–89, when he served as professor of philosophy at the University of Minnesota, Dewey spent the next 10 years at Michigan.

Philosophical Thought

Dewey left Michigan in 1894 to become professor of philosophy and chairman of the department of philosophy, psychology, and pedagogy at the University of Chicago. Dewey's achievements there brought him national fame. The increasing dominance of evolutionary biology and psychology in his thinking led him to abandon the Hegelian theory of ideas, which views them as somehow mirroring the rational order of the universe, and to accept instead an instrumentalist theory of knowledge, which conceives of ideas as tools or instruments in the solution of problems encountered in the environment. Dewey found more acceptable a theory of reality holding that nature, as encountered in scientific and ordinary experience, is the ultimate reality and man is a product of nature who finds his meaning and goals in life here and now.

Dewey's philosophical orientation has been labeled a form of pragmatism, though Dewey himself seemed to favor the term "instrumentalism," or "experimentalism." William James's *The Principles of Psychology* early stimulated Dewey's rethinking of logic and ethics by directing his attention to the practical function of ideas and concepts, but Dewey and the Chicago school of pragmatists went farther than James had gone in that they conceived of ideas as instruments for transforming the uneasiness connected with the experience of having a problem into the satisfaction of some resolution or clarification of it.

Dewey developed from these views a philosophical ground for democracy and liberalism. He conceived of democracy not as a mere form of government, but rather as a mode of association which provides the members of a society with the opportunity for maximum experimentation and personal growth. The ideal society, for Dewey, was one that provided the conditions for ever enlarging the experience of all its members.

Dewey's writings on education, notably his *The School and Society* (1899) and *The Child and the Curriculum* (1902), presented and defended what were to remain the chief underlying tenets of the philosophy of education he originated. These tenets were that the educational process must begin with and build upon the interests of the child; that it must provide opportunity for the interplay of thinking and doing in the child's classroom experience; that the teacher should be a guide and coworker with the pupils, rather than a taskmaster assigning a fixed set of lessons and recitations; and that the school's goal is the growth of the child in all aspects of its being.

Dewey's ideas and proposals strongly affected educational theory and practice in the United States. Aspects of his views were seized upon by the "progressive movement" in education, which stressed the student-centered rather than the subject-centered school, education through activity rather than through formal learning, and laboratory, workshop, or occupational education rather than the mastery of traditional subjects. But though Dewey's own faith in progressive education never wavered, he came to realize that the zeal of his followers introduced a number of excesses and defects into progressive education. Indeed, in *Experience and Education* (1938) he sharply criticized educators who sought merely to interest or amuse students, disregarded organized subject matter in favor of mere activity on the part of students, and were content with mere vocational training.

Career at Columbia University

Disagreements between President William Rainey Harper of the University of Chicago and Dewey led, in 1904, to Dewey's resignation of his posts and to his acceptance of a professorship of philosophy at Columbia University in New York City. Dewey was associated with Columbia for 47 years, first as professor and then as professor emeritus of philosophy.

His interest in current affairs prompted Dewey to contribute regularly to liberal periodicals, especially *The New Republic*. His articles focused on domestic, foreign, and international developments and were designed to reach a wide reading public. Because of his skill in analyzing and interpreting events, he soon was rated as among the best of American commentators and social critics.

ALFRED NORTH WHITEHEAD

(b. Feb. 15, 1861, Ramsgate, Isle of Thanet, Kent, Eng.—d. Dec. 30, 1947, Cambridge, Mass., U.S.)

Alfred North Whitehead was an English philosopher and mathematician who developed a comprehensive metaphysical theory from the mid-1920s. He also collaborated with Bertrand Russell on *Principia Mathematica* (1910–13).

Whitehead's father, Alfred Whitehead, an Anglican clergyman, later became vicar of Saint Peter's in Thanet. His mother, born Maria Sarah Buckmaster, was the daughter of a prosperous military tailor. Alfred North Whitehead was their youngest child.

In 1880 Whitehead entered Trinity College, Cambridge, on a scholarship. He attended only mathematical lectures, and his interests in literature, religion, philosophy, and politics were nourished solely by conversation. It was not until May 1884, however, that he was elected to an elite discussion society known as the "Apostles." Whitehead did well in the Mathematical Tripos (honors examination) of 1883–84, won a Trinity fellowship, and was appointed to the mathematical staff of the college. Stimulated by pioneering works in modern algebra, he envisaged a detailed comparative study of systems of symbolic reasoning allied to ordinary algebra. He did not begin to write his *Treatise on Universal Algebra* (1898), however, until January 1891, one month after his marriage to Evelyn Willoughby Wade.

Whitehead was at work on a second volume of his *Universal Algebra*, from 1898 to 1903, when he abandoned it because he was busy on a related, large investigation with Bertrand Russell. By the end of 1900 he had written the first draft of his brilliant *Principles of Mathematics* (1903). Whitehead agreed with its main thesis—that all pure mathematics follows from a reformed formal logic so that, of the two, logic is the fundamental discipline. By 1901 Russell had secured his collaboration on volume 2 of the *Principles*, in which this thesis was to be established by strict symbolic reasoning. The task turned out to be enormous. Their work had to be made independent of Russell's book; they called it *Principia Mathematica*. The project occupied them until 1910, when the first of its three volumes was published.

Career in London

Whitehead's future was uncertain because he had not made the sort of discoveries that cause a man to be counted an outstanding mathematician. There was, thus, little prospect of a Cambridge professorship in mathematics for him at the expiration of his Trinity lectureship. He did not wait for it to expire but moved to London in 1910, even though he had no position waiting for him there. In that first London year, Whitehead wrote the first of his books for a wide audience, *An Introduction to Mathematics* (1911), still one of the best books of its kind. In 1911 he was appointed to the staff of University College (London), and in 1914 he became professor of applied mathematics at the Imperial College of Science and Technology.

During those years, Whitehead was also constructing philosophical foundations for physics. He was led to this by the way in which he wanted to present geometry—not as deduced from hypothetical premises about assumed though imperceptible entities (e.g., points) but as the science of actual space, which is a complex of relations between extended things. From perceivable elements and relations, he logically constructed entities that are related to each other just as points are in geometry. That was only the beginning of his task, for Albert Einstein had revised the ideas of space, time, and motion. Whitehead was convinced that these three concepts should be based upon the general character of men's perception of the external world. In 1919 he published his *Enquiry Concerning the Principles of Natural Knowledge*; it was both searching and constructive but too philosophical and too complicated to influence physicists.

Career in the United States

In the early 1920s Whitehead was clearly the most distinguished philosopher of science writing in English. When a friend of Harvard University, the historical scholar Henry Osborn Taylor, pledged the money for his salary, Harvard offered Whitehead a five-year appointment as professor of philosophy.

Early in 1925, he gave a course of eight lectures in Boston, published that same year (with additions—among them his earliest writing about God) as *Science and the Modern World*. In it he dramatically described what had long engaged his meditation; namely, the rise, triumph, and impact of "scientific Materialism"—i.e., the view that nature consists of nothing else but matter in motion, or a flux of purely physical energy. He criticized this Materialism as mistaking an abstract system of mathematical physics for the concrete reality of nature.The importance of this book was immediately recognized.

Adventures of Ideas (1933) was Whitehead's last big philosophical book and the most rewarding one for the general reader. It offered penetrating, balanced reflections on the parts played by brute forces and by general ideas about humanity, God, and the universe in shaping the course of Western civilization. Whitehead emphasized the impulse of life toward newness and the absolute need for societies stable enough to nourish adventure that is fruitful rather than anarchic. In this book he also summarized his metaphysics and used it to elucidate the nature of beauty, truth, art, adventure, and peace. By "peace" he meant a religious attitude that is "primarily a trust in the efficacy of beauty."

A Fellow of the Royal Society since 1903, Whitehead was elected to the British Academy in 1931. In 1945 he received the Order of Merit. His unpublished manuscripts and correspondence were destroyed by his widow, as he had wanted.

BENEDETTO CROCE

(b. Feb. 25, 1866, Pescasseroli, Italy—d. Nov. 20, 1952, Naples)

Benedetto Croce was a historian, a humanist, and the foremost Italian philosopher of the first half of the 20th century.

Croce belonged to a family of landed proprietors with estates in the Abruzzi region of central Italy but chiefly resident in Naples. His background was religious, monarchical, and conservative. Croce spent almost his whole life in Naples, becoming intimately identified with and a keen observer of its life and a biographer of its heroes.

Founding of *La Critica*

In 1903 he founded *La Critica*, a journal of cultural criticism, in which, during the course of the next 41 years, he published nearly all his writings and reviewed all of the most important historical, philosophical, and literary work that was being produced in Europe at the time. At this same time he began the systematic exposition of his "Philosophy of the Spirit," his chief intellectual achievement. This term designates two distinct, but related, aspects of his thought. In the first aspect, philosophy of spirit designates the construction of a philosophical system on the remote pattern of the Rationalism of classical Romantic philosophy. Its principle is the "circularity" of spirit within the structure of the system and in historical time. The phases, or moments, of spirit in this system are theoretical and practical; they are distinguished, respectively, into aesthetic, logical, and economic and ethical. In the second aspect, Croce gradually abandoned, without explicitly renouncing, this schematism in response primarily to methodological considerations in history. Its moments are not dissolved but are concretized into the flow of historical action and thought. History becomes the unique mediational principle for all the moments of spirit, while spirit—i.e., human consciousness—is completely spontaneous, without a predetermined structure.

Struggle with Fascism

Croce confessed that he first saw in fascism a movement to the right of the political spectrum that might restrain and counteract the leftist tendencies toward unrestricted individual freedom released by World War I. But as the character of the Benito Mussolini regime revealed itself, his opposition hardened, becoming absolute, beyond compromise. He became, within and without Italy, the symbol of the opposition to fascism, the rallying point of the lovers of liberty.

In the maelstrom of conflict and ambiguity that followed Italy's defeat in World War II, a voice of moral authority that could speak for the true Italy was demanded. Croce's was unanimously recognized as that voice. And with authority that voice recalled Italy to the inner spiritual resources through which it might renew itself. It matters little that Croce's own project for the rebuilding of Italy—the retention of the monarchy with certain dynastic changes, the return to the principles of a revived Liberal Party in government—was not the one realized in history. More important is the fact that the new Italy, in its democratic form, was inspired by his spirit.

This last public duty fulfilled, Croce returned to his studies. In his own library—one of the finest collections in Europe within its own scope—he established the Italian Institute for Historical Studies as a research center. Asked his state of health, he replied with true stoic equanimity, "I am dying at my work." He died at age 86.

NISHIDA KITARŌ

(b. June 17, 1870, near Kanazawa, Ishikawa prefecture, Japan—d. June 7, 1945, Kamakura)

Nishida Kitarō was a Japanese philosopher who exemplified the attempt by his country to assimilate Western philosophy into the East Asian spiritual tradition.

Nishida's father, Nishida Yasunori, was for a time a teacher of an elementary school among whose few pupils was Kitarō. His mother, Tosa, was a pious devotee of the Jōdo, or True Pure Land, school of Buddhism. In his boyhood, Nishida took traditional lessons in Chinese from an excellent Confucian teacher, and in his higher school days he was taught by another scholar erudite in Chinese. Another important teacher of Nishida's was Hōjō Takiyoshi, a professor of mathematics of the Fourth Higher School, under whom Nishida had studied mathematics even before he entered high school. This exposure to Chinese culture enriched his life with a lasting Confucian quality and worldview. Later, when Western philosophy and Buddhism (especially Zen Buddhism) were merged in his mature mind, there remained deep within him an undercurrent of Confucian conviction with regard to "the ideal person," "the Way" to good and truth, sincerity, self-cultivation, and detachment.

After graduation Nishida became a teacher in a middle school near his home (1895). In the following year, he was appointed a lecturer in the Fourth Higher School at Kanazawa, and, after two years as a lecturer and later as a professor at the Yamaguchi Higher School in Yamaguchi, he was again appointed as a professor of the Fourth Higher School, teaching psychology, logic, ethics, and German (1899–1909). During his Yamaguchi and Kanazawa teaching periods, he was much engaged in the practice of Zen meditation. Remarks about Zen practice are overwhelmingly conspicuous in his diary of this period.

After one year as professor at Gakushūin University (Tokyo) in 1909, he was appointed associate professor of ethics at Kyōto Imperial University. In 1913 he was appointed professor of philosophy of religion and in 1914 professor of philosophy, a post he held until his retirement in 1928. About the end of his professorship in Kyōto Imperial University, Nishida's philosophy attained its maturity, which can be defined as "the philosophy of the *topos* (place) of Nothingness." In his latter years he delved most deeply into philosophical problems and endeavored to explain more concrete facts by his logic. Thus his idea of the true reality that overcomes the dichotomy of subjectivity and objectivity (the mind and its objects) in the *topos* of Nothingness became significant, he emphasized, for "historical reality in the historical world." Nishida developed this implication of absolute Nothingness in his *Tetsugakuron bunshū* ("Philosophical Essays"; 7 vol.), which he wrote after his retirement.

BERTRAND RUSSELL

(b. May 18, 1872, Trelleck, Monmouthshire, Wales—d. Feb. 2, 1970, Penrhyndeudraeth, Merioneth)

Bertrand Russell, a British philosopher, logician, and social reformer, was a founding figure in the analytic movement in Anglo-American (analytic) philosophy and the recipient of the Nobel Prize for Literature in 1950.

Russell was born in Ravenscroft, the country home of his parents, Lord and Lady Amberley. His grandfather, Lord John Russell, was the youngest son of the 6th Duke of Bedford. In 1861, after a long and distinguished political career in which he served twice as prime minister, Lord Russell was ennobled by Queen Victoria, becoming the 1st Earl Russell. Bertrand Russell became the 3rd Earl Russell in 1931, after his elder brother, Frank, died childless.

Russell's early life was marred by tragedy and bereavement. By the time he was age six, his sister, Rachel, his parents, and his grandfather had all died. He and Frank were left in the care of their grandmother, Countess Russell. Though Frank was sent to Winchester School, Bertrand was educated privately at home, and his childhood, to his later great regret, was spent largely in isolation from other children.

In 1890 Russell's isolation came to an end when he entered Trinity College, University of Cambridge, to study mathematics. There he made lifelong friends through his membership in the famously secretive student society the Apostles, whose members included some of the most influential philosophers of the day. Inspired by his discussions with this group, Russell abandoned mathematics for philosophy.

Analysis and Logicism

Russell flirted with idealism but soon abandoned it. His development is customarily attributed to the influence of his friend and fellow Apostle G.E. Moore. A much greater influence on his thought at this time, however, was a group of German mathematicians that included Karl Weierstrass, Georg Cantor, and Richard Dedekind, whose work was aimed at providing mathematics with a set of logically rigorous foundations. For Russell, their success in this endeavor was of enormous philosophical as well as mathematical significance; indeed, he described it as "the greatest triumph of which our age has to boast." After becoming acquainted with this body of work, Russell adopted the view, which he was to hold for the rest of his life, that analysis rather than synthesis was the surest method of philosophy, and that therefore all the grand system building of previous philosophers was misconceived.

Inspired by the work of the mathematicians whom he so greatly admired, Russell conceived the idea of demonstrating that mathematics not only had logically rigorous foundations but also that it was in its entirety nothing but logic. The philosophical case for this point of view—subsequently known as logicism—was stated at length in *The Principles of Mathematics* (1903). Near the end of his work on *The Principles of Mathematics*, Russell discovered that he had been anticipated in his logicist philosophy of mathematics by the German mathematician Gottlob Frege, whose book *The Foundations of Arithmetic* (1884) contained, as Russell put it, "many things . . . which I believed I had invented." Russell quickly added an appendix to his book that discussed Frege's work, acknowledged Frege's earlier discoveries, and explained the differences in their respective understandings of the nature of logic.

Russell's Paradox

The tragedy of Russell's intellectual life is that the deeper he thought about logic, the more his exalted conception of its significance came under threat. He himself described his philosophical development after *The Principles of Mathematics* as a "retreat from Pythagoras." The first step in this retreat was his discovery of a contradiction—now known as Russell's Paradox—at the very heart of the system of logic upon which he had hoped to build the whole of mathematics. The contradiction arises from the following considerations: Some classes are members of themselves (e.g., the class of all classes), and some are not (e.g., the class of all men), so we ought to be able to construct the class of all classes that are not members of themselves. But now, if we ask of this class "Is it a member of itself?" we become enmeshed in a contradiction. If it is, then it is not, and if it is not, then it is. This is rather like defining the village barber as "the man who shaves all those who do not shave themselves" and then asking whether the barber shaves himself or not.

At first this paradox seemed trivial, but the more Russell reflected upon it, the deeper the problem seemed, and eventually he was persuaded that there was something fundamentally wrong with the notion of class as he had understood it in *The Principles of Mathematics*. Frege saw the depth of the problem immediately. When Russell wrote to him to tell him of the paradox, Frege replied, "arithmetic totters." The foundation upon which Frege and Russell had hoped to build mathematics had, it seemed, collapsed. Whereas Frege sank into a deep depression, Russell set about repairing the damage by attempting to construct a theory of logic immune to the paradox. Like a malignant cancerous growth, however, the contradiction reappeared in different guises whenever Russell thought that he had eliminated it.

Eventually, Russell's attempts to overcome the paradox resulted in a complete transformation of his scheme of logic, as he added one refinement after another to the basic theory. In the process, important elements of his "Pythagorean" view of logic were abandoned. In particular, Russell came to the conclusion that there were no such things as classes and propositions and that therefore, whatever logic was, it was not the study of them. In their place he substituted a bewilderingly complex theory known as the ramified theory of types, which, though it successfully avoided contradictions such as Russell's Paradox, was (and remains) extraordinarily difficult to understand. By the time he and his collaborator, Alfred North Whitehead, had finished the three volumes of *Principia Mathematica* (1910–13), the theory of types and other innovations to the basic logical system had made it unmanageably complicated.

Despite their differences, Russell and Frege were alike in taking an essentially Platonic view of logic. Indeed, the passion with which Russell pursued the project of deriving mathematics from logic owed a great deal to what he would later somewhat scornfully describe as a "kind of mathematical mysticism." As he put it in his more disillusioned old age, "I disliked the real world and sought refuge in a timeless world, without change or decay or the will-o'-the-wisp of progress." Russell, like Pythagoras and Plato before him, believed that there existed a realm of truth that, unlike the messy contingencies of the everyday world of sense-experience, was immutable and eternal. This realm was accessible only to reason, and knowledge of it, once attained, was not tentative or corrigible but certain and irrefutable. Logic, for Russell, was the means by which one gained access to this realm, and thus the pursuit of logic was, for him, the highest and noblest enterprise life had to offer.

Theory of Descriptions and Later Doctrines

In philosophy, the greatest impact of *Principia Mathematica* has been through its so-called theory of descriptions. This method of analysis, first introduced by Russell in his article "On Denoting" (1905), translates propositions containing definite descriptions (e.g., "the present king of France") into expressions that do not—the purpose being to remove the logical awkwardness of appearing to refer to things (such as the present king of France) that do not exist. Originally developed by Russell as part of his efforts to overcome the contradictions in his theory of logic, this method of analysis has since become widely influential even among philosophers with no specific interest in mathematics. The general idea at the root of Russell's theory of descriptions—that the grammatical structures of ordinary language are distinct from, and often conceal, the true "logical forms" of expressions—has become his most enduring contribution to philosophy.

Russell later said that his mind never fully recovered from the strain of writing *Principia Mathematica*, and he never again worked on logic with quite the same intensity. In 1918 he wrote *An Introduction to Mathematical Philosophy*, which was intended as a popularization of *Principia*, but, apart from this, his philosophical work tended to be on epistemology rather than logic. In 1914, in *Our Knowledge of the External World*, Russell argued that the world is "constructed" out of sense-data, an idea that he refined in *The Philosophy of Logical Atomism* (1918–19). In *The Analysis of Mind* (1921) and *The Analysis of Matter* (1927), he abandoned this notion in favor of what he called neutral monism, the view that the "ultimate stuff" of the world is neither mental nor physical but something "neutral" between the two. Although treated with respect, these works had markedly less impact upon subsequent philosophers than his early works in logic and the philosophy of mathematics, and they are generally regarded as inferior by comparison.

A Turbulent Life

Connected with the change in his intellectual direction after the completion of *Principia* was a profound change in his personal life. Throughout the years that he worked single-mindedly on logic, Russell's private life was bleak and joyless. He had fallen out of love with his first wife, Alys, though he continued to live with her. In 1911, however, he fell passionately in love with Lady Ottoline Morrell. Doomed from the start (because Morrell had no intention of leaving her husband), this love nevertheless transformed Russell's entire life. He left Alys and began to hope that he might, after all, find fulfillment in romance.

In the same year that he began his affair with Morrell, Russell met Ludwig Wittgenstein, a brilliant young Austrian who arrived at Cambridge to study logic with Russell. Fired with intense enthusiasm for the subject, Wittgenstein made great progress, and within a year Russell began to look to him to provide the next big step in philosophy and to defer to him on questions of logic. However, Wittgenstein's own work, eventually published in 1921 as *Logisch-philosophische Abhandlung* (*Tractatus Logico-Philosophicus*, 1922), undermined the entire approach to logic that had inspired Russell's great contributions to the philosophy of mathematics. It persuaded Russell that there were no "truths" of logic at all, that logic consisted entirely of tautologies, the truth of which was not guaranteed by eternal facts in the Platonic realm of ideas but lay, rather, simply in the nature of language. This was to be the final step in the retreat from Pythagoras and a further incentive for Russell to abandon technical philosophy in favor of other pursuits.

During World War I Russell was for a while a full-time political agitator, campaigning for peace and against conscription. He was twice taken to court, the second time to receive a sentence of six months in prison, which he served at the end of the war. In 1916, as a result of his antiwar campaigning, Russell was dismissed from his lectureship at Trinity College. The war had had a profound effect on Russell's political views, causing him to abandon his inherited liberalism and to adopt a thorough-going socialism.

In 1921 Russell married his second wife, Dora Black, a young graduate of Girton College, Cambridge, with whom he had two children, John and Kate. In the interwar years Russell and Dora acquired a reputation as leaders of a progressive socialist movement that was stridently anticlerical, openly defiant of conventional sexual morality, and dedicated to educational reform. Russell's published work during this period consists mainly of journalism and popular books written in support of these causes. His public lecture "Why I Am Not a Christian," delivered in 1927 and printed many times, became a popular locus classicus of atheistic rationalism. In 1927 Russell and Dora set up their own school, Beacon Hill, as a pioneering experiment in primary education.

In 1932 Russell left Dora for Patricia ("Peter") Spence, a young University of Oxford undergraduate, and for the next three years his life was dominated by an extraordinarily acrimonious and complicated divorce from

Dora, which was finally granted in 1935. In the following year he married Spence, and in 1937 they had a son, Conrad.

Return to Academia

Worn out by years of frenetic public activity and desiring, at this comparatively late stage in his life (he was then age 66), to return to academic philosophy, Russell gained a teaching post at the University of Chicago. From 1938 to 1944 Russell lived in the United States, where he taught at Chicago and the University of California at Los Angeles, but he was prevented from taking a post at the City College of New York because of objections to his views on sex and marriage. On the brink of financial ruin, he secured a job teaching the history of philosophy at the Barnes Foundation in Philadelphia. Although he soon fell out with its founder, Albert C. Barnes, and lost his job, Russell was able to turn the lectures he delivered at the foundation into a book, *A History of Western Philosophy* (1945), which proved to be a bestseller and was for many years his main source of income.

In 1944 Russell returned to Trinity College, where he lectured on the ideas that formed his last major contribution to philosophy, *Human Knowledge: Its Scope and Limits* (1948). During this period Russell, for once in his life, found favor with the authorities. He received many official tributes, including the Order of Merit in 1949 and the Nobel Prize for Literature in 1950. His private life, however, remained as turbulent as ever, and he left his third wife in 1949.

In 1952 Russell married his fourth wife, Edith Finch, and finally, at the age of 80, found lasting marital harmony. Russell devoted his last years to campaigning against nuclear weapons and the Vietnam War, assuming once again the role of gadfly of the establishment.

G. E. MOORE

(b. Nov. 4, 1873, London, Eng.—d. Oct. 24, 1958, Cambridge, Cambridgeshire)

G. E. (George Edward) Moore was an influential British Realist philosopher and professor whose systematic approach to ethical problems and remarkably meticulous approach to philosophy made him an outstanding modern British thinker.

Elected to a fellowship at Trinity College, Cambridge, in 1898, Moore remained there until 1904, during which time he published several journal articles, including "The Nature of Judgment" (1899) and "The Refutation of Idealism" (1903), as well as his major ethical work, *Principia Ethica* (1903). These writings were important in helping to undermine the influence of Hegel and Kant on British philosophy. After residence in Edinburgh and London, he returned to Cambridge in 1911 to become a lecturer in moral science. From 1925 to 1939 he was professor of philosophy there, and from 1921 to 1947 he was editor of the philosophical journal *Mind*.

A friend of Bertrand Russell, who first directed him to the study of philosophy, Moore was also a leading figure in the Bloomsbury group, a coterie that included the economist John Keynes and the writers Virginia Woolf and E. M. Forster. Because of his view that "the good" is knowable by direct apprehension, he became known as an "ethical intuitionist." He claimed that other efforts to decide what is "good," such as analyses of the concepts of approval or desire, which are not themselves of an ethical nature, partake of a fallacy that he termed the "naturalistic fallacy."

Moore was also preoccupied with such problems as the nature of sense perception and the existence of other minds and material things. He was not as skeptical as those philosophers who held that we lack sufficient data to prove that objects exist outside our own minds, but he did believe that proper philosophical proofs had not yet been devised to overcome such objections.

Although few of Moore's theories achieved general acceptance, his unique approaches to certain problems and his intellectual rigor helped change the texture of philosophical discussion in England. His other major writings include *Philosophical Studies* (1922) and *Some Main Problems of Philosophy* (1953); posthumous publications were *Philosophical Papers* (1959) and the *Commonplace Book, 1919–1953* (1962).

MARTIN BUBER

(b. Feb. 8, 1878, Vienna, Austria-Hungary [now in Austria]—d. June 13, 1965, Jerusalem, Israel)

German-Jewish Martin Buber was a religious philosopher, biblical translator and interpreter, and master of German prose style. His philosophy was centered on the encounter, or dialogue, of the individual with other beings, particularly exemplified in the relation with other persons but ultimately resting on and pointing to the relation with God. This thought reached its fullest dialogical expression in *Ich und Du* (1923; *I and Thou*).

From Vienna to Jerusalem

Buber was the son of Carl Buber, an agronomist, and his wife—both assimilated Jews. When Martin was three his mother left his father, and the boy was brought up by his grandparents in Lemberg (now Lviv, Ukraine). The search after the lost mother became a strong motive for his dialogical thinking—his I-Thou philosophy.

Buber's grammar-school education provided him with an excellent grounding in the classics. During his adolescence he ceased to participate in Jewish religious observances. In his university days—he attended the universities of Vienna, Berlin, Leipzig, and Zürich—Buber studied philosophy and art. His doctoral dissertation (*Vienna*, 1904) dealt with the theories of individuation in the thought of two great mystics, Nicholas of Cusa and Jakob Böhme, but it was Friedrich Nietzsche's proclamation of heroic nihilism and his criticism of modern culture that exerted the greatest influence on Buber at that time. The Nietzschean influence was reflected in Buber's turn to Zionism and its call for a return to roots and a more wholesome culture.

In 1916 Buber founded the influential monthly *Der Jude* ("The Jew"), which he edited until 1924 and which became the central forum for practically all German-reading Jewish intellectuals. In its pages he advocated the unpopular cause of Jewish-Arab cooperation in the formation of a binational state in Palestine.

After his marriage (1901) to a non-Jewish, pro-Zionist author, Paula Winckler, who converted to Judaism, Buber took up the study of Hasidism. His *Chassidischen Bücher* (1927) made the legacy of this popular 18th-century eastern European Jewish pietistic movement a part of Western literature. In Hasidism Buber saw a healing power for the malaise of Judaism and mankind in an age of alienation that had shaken three vital human relationships: those between man and God, man and man, and man and nature. They can be restored, he asserted, only by man's again meeting the other person or being who stands over against him, on all three levels—the divine, human, and natural. Buber maintained that early Hasidism accomplished this encounter and that Zionism should follow its example.

Buber's pedagogical work reached a climax under the new conditions created by the Nazi assumption of power. In November 1933 he became head of the newly reopened Freies Jüdisches Lehrhaus for Jewish adult education in Frankfurt am Main. In 1934 he became director of the whole organization of Jewish adult education and retraining of Jewish teachers in Nazi Germany, where Jewish teachers and students were being progressively excluded from the educational system. He was a courageous spokesman of spiritual resistance.

After the Nazi secret police forbade his public lectures and then all of his teaching activities, he emigrated as a man of 60 to Palestine. He was appointed to a professorship in social philosophy at Hebrew University in Jerusalem, a post he held until 1951. He was the first president of the Israeli Academy of Sciences and Arts. After the establishment of the State of Israel, Buber initiated the founding of the Teachers Training College for Adult Education in Jerusalem and became its head (1949).

From Mysticism to Dialogue

Buber's manifold activities were inspired by his philosophy of encounter—of man's meeting with other beings. An early mystical period culminated in *Daniel* (1913), five dialogues on orientation and realization, man's two basic stances toward the world. Orientation takes the world as a static state of affairs governed by comprehensible laws. It is a receptive, analytical, or systematizing attitude. Realization, on the other hand, is a creative, participative attitude that realizes the possibilities in things, experiencing through one's own full reality the full reality of the world. It operates within an open horizon of possibilities.

The *Reden über das Judentum* (1923; "Talks on Judaism") mark another step in his development. The early "Talks" were delivered in 1909–11 before large Zionist student audiences in Prague; each of the speeches tries to answer its opening question: "Jews, why do we call ourselves Jews?" To half-assimilated Zionists in search of a rationale for their Jewish existence, Buber offered his theories regarding the essence of Judaism, basing his quest for it on his listeners' assumed identity as Jews. In some of the "Talks," as well as in *Daniel*, the mystic element still prevails, but Buber later abandoned the notion of a mystical union between man and God and embraced instead the notion of their encounter, which presupposes and preserves their separate existence.

This basic view underlies Buber's mature thinking; it was expressed with great philosophic and poetic power in his famous work *Ich und Du* (1923; *I and Thou*). According to this view, God, the great Thou, enables human I–Thou relations between man and other beings. Their measure of mutuality is related to the levels of being: it is almost nil on the inorganic and botanic levels, rare on the animal level, but always possible and sometimes actual between human beings. A true relationship with God, as experienced from the human side, must be an I–Thou relationship, in which God is truly met and addressed, not merely thought of and expressed.

Between man and man, the I–Thou relationship into which both parties enter in the fullness of their being—as in a great love at its highest moment or in an ideal friendship—is an exception. Generally, we enter into relationships not with the fullness of our being but only with some fraction of it. This is the I–It relationship, as in scholarly pursuits in which other beings are reduced to mere objects of thought or in social relations (e.g., boss and worker) wherein persons are treated largely as tools or conveniences. This form of relationship enables the creation of pure and applied science as well as the manipulation of man by man. Buber's ethical concept of the demarcation line—to be drawn anew every day between the maximum of good that can be done in a concrete situation and the minimum of evil that must be done in it—calls for an I–Thou relation whenever possible and settles for an I–It relation whenever necessary—e.g., for the purpose of human survival.

Final Years

In his last years a group of kibbutz members turned to him with their personal and communal problems. *Siḥot loḥamin* (1967; *The Seventh Day*, 1970), published by them shortly after the Six-Day War, testifies to Buber's living spirit by its self-searching attitude on ethical questions of war and peace and on Arab–Jewish relations.

An unprecedented event occurred at Buber's funeral in Jerusalem, a high state function. A delegation of the Arab Students' Organization placed a wreath on the grave of one who strove mightily for peace between Israel's and Palestine's two peoples.

LUDWIG WITTGENSTEIN

(b. April 26, 1889, Vienna, Austria-Hungary [now in Austria]—d. April 29, 1951, Cambridge, Cambridgeshire, Eng.)

Ludwig Wittgenstein was an Austrian-born English philosopher who has been regarded by many as the greatest philosopher of the 20th century. His charismatic personality has, in addition, exerted a powerful fascination upon artists, playwrights, poets, novelists, musicians, and even filmmakers, so that his fame has spread far beyond the confines of academic life.

Wittgenstein was born into one of the wealthiest and most remarkable families of Habsburg Vienna. His father, Karl Wittgenstein, was an industrialist of extraordinary talent and energy who rose to become one of the leading figures in the Austrian iron and steel industry. Although his family was originally Jewish, Karl Wittgenstein had been brought up as a Protestant, and his wife, Leopoldine, also from a partly Jewish family, had been raised as a Catholic. Karl and Leopoldine had eight children, of whom Ludwig was the youngest. The family possessed both money and talent in abundance, and their home became a center of Viennese cultural life during one of its most dynamic phases. Leopoldine Wittgenstein played the piano to a remarkably high standard, as did many of her children. One of them, Paul, became a famous concert pianist, and another, Hans, was regarded as a musical prodigy comparable to Mozart. But the family also was beset with tragedy. Three of Ludwig's brothers—Hans, Rudolf, and Kurt—committed suicide, the first two after rebelling against their father's wish that they pursue careers in industry.

Although he shared his family's veneration for music, Wittgenstein's deepest interest as a boy was in engineering. In 1908 he went to Manchester, England, to study the then-nascent subject of aeronautics. While engaged on a project to design a jet propeller, Wittgenstein became increasingly absorbed in purely mathematical problems. After reading *The Principles of Mathematics* (1903) by Bertrand Russell and *The Foundations of Arithmetic* (1884) by Gottlob Frege, he developed an obsessive interest in the philosophy of logic and mathematics. In 1911 Wittgenstein went to Trinity College, University of Cambridge, in order to make Russell's acquaintance. From the moment he met Russell, Wittgenstein's aeronautical studies were forgotten in favor of a ferociously intense preoccupation with questions of logic.

Wittgenstein worked with such intensity on logic that within a year Russell declared that he had nothing left to teach him. Wittgenstein evidently thought so too and left Cambridge to work on his own in remote isolation in a wooden hut that he built by the side of a fjord in Norway. There he developed, in embryo, what became known as the picture theory of meaning, a central tenet of which is that a proposition can express a fact by virtue of sharing with it a common structure or "logical form." This logical form, however, precisely because it is what makes "picturing" possible, cannot itself be pictured. It follows both that logic is inexpressible and that there are—pace Frege and Russell—no logical facts or logical truths. Logical form has to be shown rather than stated, and, though some languages and methods of symbolism might reveal their structure more perspicuously than others, there is no symbolism capable of representing its own structure.

The Tractatus Logico-Philosophicus

In the summer of 1914, at the outbreak of World War I, Wittgenstein was staying with his family in Vienna. Unable to return to Norway to continue his work on logic, he enlisted in the Austrian army. Wittgenstein spent the first two years of the war behind the lines, relatively safe from harm and able to continue his work on logic. In 1916, however, at his own request, he was sent to a fighting unit at the Russian front. His surviving manuscripts show that during this time his philosophical work underwent a profound change. Whereas previously he had separated his thoughts on logic from his thoughts on ethics, aesthetics, and religion by writing the latter remarks in code, at this point he began to integrate the two sets of remarks, applying to all of them the distinction he had earlier made between that which can be said and that which must be shown. Ethics, aesthetics, and religion, in other words, were like logic: their "truths" were inexpressible; insight in these areas could be shown but not stated.

Near the end of the war, while he was on leave in Salzburg, Austria, Wittgenstein finally finished the book that was later published as *Tractatus Logico-Philosophicus*. In the preface he announced that he considered himself to have found "on all essential points" the solution to the problems of philosophy. For the most part, the book consists of an austerely compressed exposition of the picture theory of meaning. It ends, however, with some remarks about ethics, aesthetics, and the meaning of life, stressing that, if its view about how propositions can be meaningful is correct, then, just as there are no meaningful propositions about logical form, so there can be no meaningful propositions concerning these subjects either. This point, of course, applies to Wittgenstein's own remarks in the book itself, so Wittgenstein is forced to conclude that whoever understands his remarks "finally recognizes them as senseless"; they offer, so to speak, a ladder that one must throw away after using it to climb.

Consistent with his view that he had solved all the essential problems of philosophy, Wittgenstein abandoned the subject after World War I and instead trained to be an elementary school teacher. Meanwhile, the *Tractatus* was published and attracted the attention of two influential groups of philosophers, one based in Cambridge and including R. B. Braithwaite and Frank Ramsey and the other based in Vienna and including Moritz Schlick, Friedrich Waismann, and other logical positivists later collectively known as the Vienna Circle. Both groups tried to make contact with Wittgenstein. Frank Ramsey made

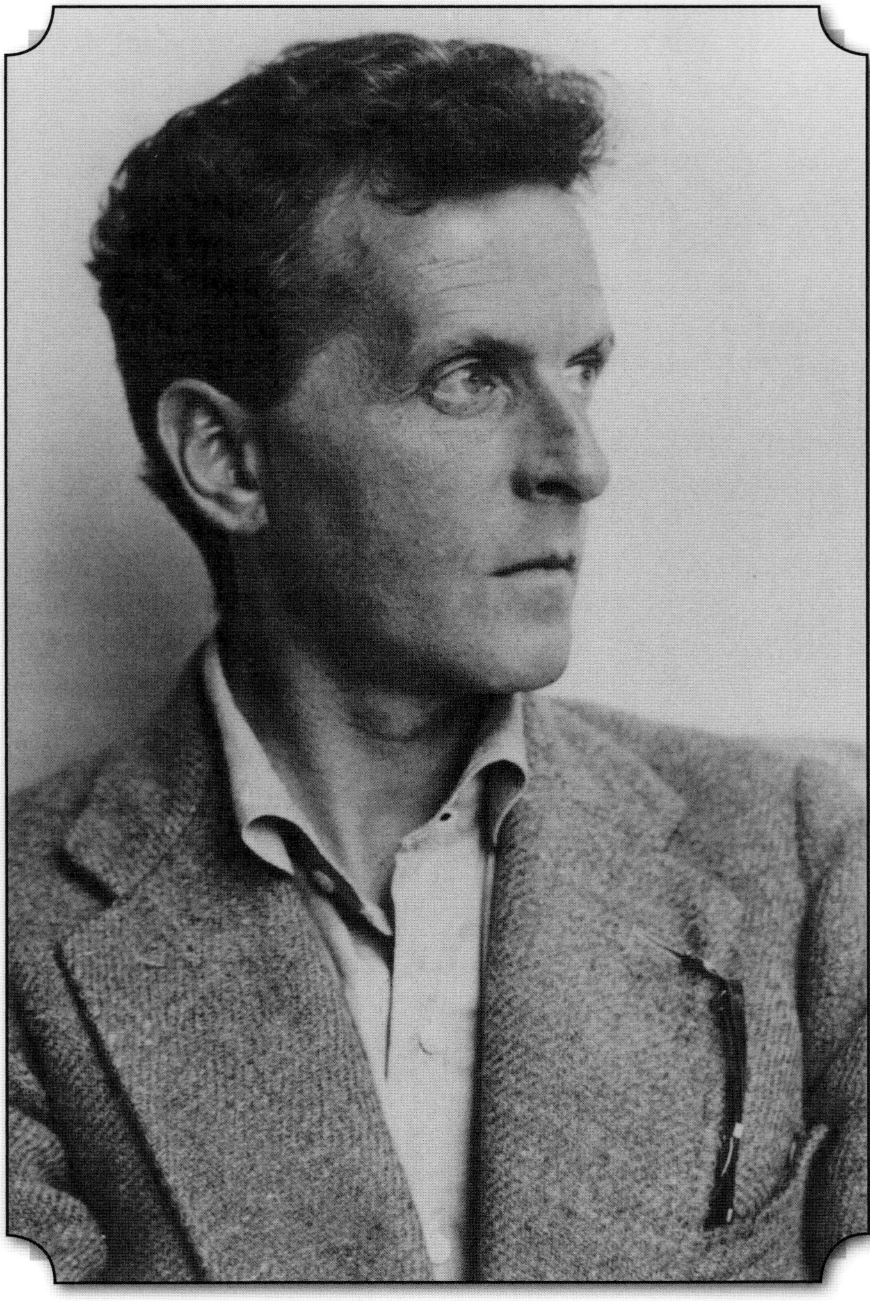

Ludwig Wittgenstein is often considered to be the greatest philosopher of the 20th century, with wide-ranging influence beyond the field of philosophy.

two trips to Puchberg—the small Austrian village in which Wittgenstein was teaching—to discuss the *Tractatus* with him, and Schlick invited him to join the discussions of the Vienna Circle. Stimulated by these contacts, Wittgenstein's interest in philosophy revived, and, after his brief and unsuccessful career as a schoolteacher came to an end, he returned to the discipline, persuaded, largely by Ramsey, that the views he had expressed in his book were not, after all, definitively correct.

A New Understanding of Philosophy

In 1929 Wittgenstein returned to Trinity College, initially to work with Ramsey. The following year Ramsey died at the tragically young age of 26, after a spell of severe jaundice. Wittgenstein stayed on at Cambridge as a lecturer, spending his vacations in Vienna. During this time his ideas changed rapidly as he abandoned altogether the notion of logical form as it appeared in the *Tractatus*, along with the theory of meaning that it had seemed to require. Indeed, he adopted a view of philosophy that rejected entirely the construction of theories of any sort and that viewed philosophy rather as an activity, a method of clearing up the confusions that arise through misunderstandings of language.

Philosophers, Wittgenstein believed, had been misled into thinking that their subject was a kind of science, a search for theoretical explanations of the things that puzzled them: the nature of meaning, truth, mind, time, justice, and so on. But philosophical problems are not amenable to this kind of treatment, he claimed. What is required is not a correct doctrine but a clear view, one that dispels the confusion that gives rise to the problem. Many of these problems arise through an inflexible view of language that insists that if a word has a meaning there must be some kind of object corresponding to it. If we remind ourselves that language has many uses and that words can be used quite meaningfully without corresponding to things, the problem disappears.

Wittgenstein thought that he himself had succumbed to an overly narrow view of language in the *Tractatus*, concentrating on the question of how propositions acquired their meaning and ignoring all other aspects of meaningful language use. A proposition is something that is either true or false, but we do not use language only to say things that are true or false, and thus a theory of propositions is not—pace the *Tractatus*—a general theory of meaning nor even the basis of one.

Wittgenstein found the proper arrangement of his later book, *Philosophical Investigations*, enormously difficult. For the last 20 years of his life, he tried again and again to produce a version of the book that satisfied him, but he never felt he had succeeded, and he would not allow the book to be published in his lifetime. What became known as the works of the later Wittgenstein are the discarded attempts at a definitive expression of his new approach to philosophy.

The themes addressed by Wittgenstein in these posthumously published manuscripts and typescripts are so various as to defy summary. The two focal points are the traditional problems in the philosophy of mathematics (e.g., "What is mathematical truth?" and "What are numbers?") and the problems that arise from thinking about the mind (e.g., "What is consciousness?" and "What is a soul?"). Wittgenstein's method is not to engage directly in polemics against specific philosophical theories but rather to trace their source in confusions about language.

To dispel these confusions, Wittgenstein developed

a method of describing and imagining what he called "language games." Language games, for Wittgenstein, are concrete social activities that crucially involve the use of specific forms of language. By describing the countless variety of language games—the countless ways in which language is actually used in human interaction—Wittgenstein meant to show that "the speaking of a language is part of an activity, or of a form of life." The meaning of a word, then, is not the object to which it corresponds but rather the use that is made of it in "the stream of life."

Last Years

Wittgenstein himself several times considered leaving his academic job in favor of training to become a psychiatrist. In 1935 he even thought seriously of moving to the Soviet Union to work on a farm. When he was offered the prestigious chair of philosophy at Cambridge in 1939, he accepted, but with severe misgivings. During World War II he worked as a porter in Guy's Hospital in London and then as an assistant in a medical research team.

In 1947 he finally resigned his academic position and moved to Ireland to work on his own, as he had done in Norway before World War I. In 1949 he discovered that he had cancer of the prostate, and in 1951 he moved into his doctor's house in Cambridge, knowing that he had only a few months to live. He died on April 29, 1951. His last words were: "Tell them I've had a wonderful life."

MARTIN HEIDEGGER

(b. Sept. 26, 1889, Messkirch, Schwarzwald, Ger.—d. May 26, 1976, Messkirch, W. Ger.)

Martin Heidegger, a German philosopher, was one of the main exponents of Existentialism. His groundbreaking work in ontology and metaphysics determined the course of 20th-century philosophy on the European continent and exerted an enormous influence in virtually every other humanistic discipline, including literary criticism, hermeneutics, psychology, and theology.

Background and Youth

The son of a Roman Catholic sexton, Heidegger showed an early interest in religion. Intending to become a priest, he began theological studies at the University of Freiburg in 1909 but switched to philosophy and mathematics in 1911.

Franz Brentano's work in ontology helped to inspire Heidegger's lifelong conviction that there is a single, basic sense of the verb "to be" that lies behind all its varied usages. From Brentano Heidegger also developed his enthusiasm for the ancient Greeks—especially the pre-Socratics. In addition to these philosophers, Heidegger's work is obviously influenced by Plato, Aristotle, the Gnostic philosophers of the 2nd century CE, and several 19th- and early 20th-century thinkers, including the early figures of Existentialism, Søren Kierkegaard and Friedrich Nietzsche; Wilhelm Dilthey, who was noted for directing the attention of philosophers to the human and historical sciences; and Edmund Husserl, the founder of the phenomenological movement in philosophy.

While still in his 20s, Heidegger studied at Freiburg with Heinrich Rickert, the leading figure of the axiological school of neo-Kantianism, and with Husserl, who was then already famous. Husserl's phenomenology, and especially his struggle against the intrusion of psychologism into traditionally philosophical studies of man, determined the background of the young Heidegger's doctoral dissertation, *Die Lehre vom Urteil im Psychologismus: Ein kritisch-positiver Beitrag zur Logik* ("The Doctrine of Judgment in Psychologism: A Critical-Positive Contribution to Logic"; 1914).

Philosophy

Heidegger began teaching at the University of Freiburg during the winter semester of 1915 and wrote his habilitation thesis on the 13th-century English Franciscan philosopher Duns Scotus. As a colleague of Husserl, Heidegger was expected to carry the phenomenological movement forward in the spirit of his former master. As a religiously inclined young man, however, he went his own way instead. While serving as a professor ordinarius at Marburg University (1923–28), he astonished the German philosophical world with *Being and Time* (1927). Although almost unreadable, it was immediately felt to be of prime importance, whatever its relation to Husserl might be. In spite of—and perhaps partly because of—its intriguingly difficult style, *Being and Time* was acclaimed as a masterpiece not only in German-speaking countries but also in Latin ones, where phenomenology was well established. It strongly influenced Jean-Paul Sartre and other existentialists in France, and on the basis of this work Heidegger came to be regarded as the leading atheistic Existentialist, though he always rejected that label. The reception of *Being and Time* in the English-speaking world was chilly, however, and its influence there was negligible for several decades.

Heidegger's declared purpose in *Being and Time* is to show what it means for a person to be—or, more accurately, how it is for a person to be. This task leads to a more fundamental question: what does it mean to ask, "What is the meaning of Being?" These questions lie behind the obviousness of everyday life and, therefore, also behind the empirical questions of natural science. They are usually overlooked, because they are too near to everyday life to be grasped. One might say that Heidegger's entire prophetic mission amounts to making each person ask this question with maximum involvement. Whether one arrives at a definite answer is, in the present crisis of mankind, of secondary importance.

The wealth of ideas in *Being and Time* is best discussed in conjunction with those developed in another, shorter work, *What Is Metaphysics?* (1929), which was originally delivered as an inaugural lecture when Heidegger succeeded Husserl at Freiburg in 1928. As Heidegger learned from Husserl, it is the phenomenological and not the scientific method that unveils man's ways of Being. Thus, in pursuing this method, Heidegger comes into conflict with the dichotomy of the subject-object relation, which has traditionally implied that man, as knower, is something (some-thing) within an environment that is against him. This relation, however, must be transcended. The deepest knowing, on the contrary, is a matter of *phainesthai* (Greek: "to show itself" or "to be in the light"), the word from which phenomenology, as a method, is derived. Something is just "there" in the light. Thus, the distinction between subject and object is not immediate but comes only later through conceptualization, as in the sciences.

In the early 1930s Heidegger's thought underwent a change that scholars call his *Kehre* ("turning around"). Although some specialists regard the *Kehre* as a turning away from the central problem of *Being and Time*, Heidegger himself denied this, insisting that he had been asking the same basic question since his youth. Nevertheless, in his later years he clearly became more reluctant to offer an answer, or even to indicate a way in which an answer might be found.

Heidegger and Nazism

In the months after the appointment of Adolf Hitler as chancellor of Germany in January 1933, German universities came under increasing pressure to support the "national revolution" and to eliminate Jewish scholars and the teaching of "Jewish" doctrines, such as the theory of relativity. After the rector of Freiburg resigned to protest these policies, the university's teaching staff elected Heidegger as his successor in April 1933. One month later, Heidegger became a member of the Nazi Party, and until he resigned as rector in April 1934 he helped to institute Nazi educational and cultural programs at Freiburg and vigorously promoted the domestic and foreign policies of the Nazi regime. In the fall of 1933, Heidegger began a speaking tour on behalf of Hitler's national referendum to withdraw Germany from the League of Nations. As he proclaimed in one speech: "Let not doctrines and ideas be your guide. The Führer is Germany's only reality and law." Heidegger continued to support Hitler in the years after his rectorship, though with somewhat less enthusiasm than he had shown in 1933–34.

At the end of the war in 1945, a favorably disposed university de-Nazification commission found Heidegger guilty of having "consciously placed the great prestige of his scholarly reputation . . . in the service of the National Socialist Revolution," and he was banned from further teaching. (The ban was lifted in 1950.) In later years, despite pleas from friends and associates to disavow publicly his Nazi past, Heidegger declined to do so. In his book *Introduction to Metaphysics*, published in 1953, Heidegger retrospectively praised "the inner truth and greatness of National Socialism." Beginning in the 1980s, there was considerable controversy among Heidegger scholars regarding the alleged connection between Heidegger's philosophy and his political views in the 1930s and '40s.

RUDOLF CARNAP

(b. May 18, 1891, Ronsdorf, Ger.—d. Sept. 14, 1970, Santa Monica, Calif., U.S.)

Rudolf Carnap was a German-born U.S. philosopher of Logical Positivism. He made important contributions to logic, the analysis of language, the theory of probability, and the philosophy of science.

From 1910 to 1914, Carnap studied mathematics, physics, and philosophy at the universities of Jena and Freiburg im Breisgau. At Jena he attended the lectures of Gottlob Frege, now widely acknowledged as the greatest logician of the 19th century, whose ideas exerted a deep influence on Carnap.

After serving in World War I, Carnap earned his doctorate in 1921 at Jena with a dissertation on the concept of space. He argued that the conflicts among the various theories of space then held by scholars resulted from the fact that those theories actually dealt with quite different subjects; he called them, respectively, formal space, physical space, and intuitive space and exhibited their principal characteristics and fundamental differences.

For several years afterward Carnap was engaged in

private research in logic and the foundations of physics and wrote a number of essays on problems of space, time, and causality, as well as a textbook in symbolic, or mathematical, logic (*Abriss der Logistik*, 1929; a considerably different later German version appeared in English translation: *Introduction to Symbolic Logic and Its Applications*, 1958).

Logical Empiricism

In 1926 Moritz Schlick, the founder of the Vienna Circle—a small group of philosophers, mathematicians, and other scholars who met regularly to discuss philosophical issues—invited Carnap to join the faculty of the University of Vienna, where he soon became an influential member of the Circle. Out of their discussions developed the initial ideas of Logical Positivism, or Logical Empiricism. This school of thought shared its basic Empiricist orientation with David Hume, a Scottish Empiricist, and Ernst Mach, an Austrian physicist and philosopher. Its leading members, informed and inspired by the methods and theories of contemporary mathematics and science, sought to develop a "scientific world view" by bringing to philosophical inquiry the precision and rigor of the exact sciences. As one means to this end, Carnap made extensive use of the concepts and techniques of symbolic logic in preference to the often inadequate analytic devices of traditional logic.

Carnap and his associates established close connections with like-minded scholars in other countries, among them a group of Empiricists that had formed in Berlin under the leadership of Hans Reichenbach, an eminent philosopher of science. With Reichenbach, Carnap founded a periodical, *Erkenntnis* (1930–40), as a forum for the new "scientific philosophy."

The basic thesis of Empiricism, in a familiar but quite vague formulation, is that all of man's concepts and beliefs concerning the world ultimately derive from his immediate experience. In some of his most important writings, Carnap sought, in effect, to give this idea a clear and precise interpretation. Setting aside, as a psychological rather than a philosophical problem, the question of how human beings arrive at their ideas about the world, he proceeded to construe Empiricism as a systematic-logical thesis about the evidential grounding of empirical knowledge. To this end, he gave the issue a characteristically linguistic turn by asking how the terms and sentences that, in scientific or in everyday language, serve to express assertions about the world are related to those terms and sentences by which the data of immediate experience can be described. The Empiricist thesis, as construed and defended by Carnap, then asserts that the terms and sentences of the first kind are "reducible" to those of the second kind in a clearly specifiable sense. Carnap's conception of the relevant sense of reducibility, which he always stated in precise logical terms, was initially rather narrow but gradually became more liberal.

Works on Empiricism

In his first great work, *Der logische Aufbau der Welt* (1928; *The Logical Structure of the World: Pseudoproblems in Philosophy*), Carnap developed, with unprecedented rigor, a version of the Empiricist reducibility thesis according to which all terms suited to describe actual or possible empirical facts are fully definable by terms referring exclusively to aspects of immediate experience, so that all empirical statements are fully translatable into statements about immediate experiences.

Prompted by discussions with his associates in Vienna, Carnap soon began to develop a more liberal version of Empiricism, which he elaborated while he was professor of natural philosophy at the German University in Prague (1931–35). He eventually presented it in full detail in his essay "Testability and Meaning" (*Philosophy of Science*, vol. 3 [1936] and 4 [1937]). Carnap argued that the terms of empirical science are not fully definable in purely experiential terms but can at least be partly defined by means of "reduction sentences," which are logically much-refined versions of operational definitions, and "observation sentences," whose truth can be checked by direct observation. Carnap stressed that usually such tests cannot provide strict proof or disproof but only more or less strong "confirmation" for an empirical statement.

Sentences that do not thus yield observational implications and therefore cannot possibly be tested and confirmed by observational findings were said to be empirically meaningless. By reference to this testability criterion of empirical significance, Carnap and other Logical Empiricists rejected various doctrines of speculative metaphysics and of theology, not as being false but as making no significant assertions at all.

Carnap argued that the observational statements by reference to which empirical statements can be tested may be construed as sentences describing directly and publicly observable aspects of physical objects, such as the needle of a measuring instrument turning to a particular point on the scale or a subject in a psychological test showing a change in pulse rate. All such sentences, he noted, can be formulated in terms that are part of the vocabulary of physics. This was the basic idea of his "physicalism," according to which all terms and statements of empirical science—from the physical to the social and historical disciplines—can be reduced to terms and statements in the language of physics.

In later writings, Carnap liberalized his conception of reducibility and of empirical significance even further so as to give a more adequate account of the relation between scientific theories and scientific evidence.

Career in the United States

By the time "Testability and Meaning" appeared in print, Carnap had moved to the United States, mainly because of the growing threat of German National Socialism. From 1936 to 1952 he served on the faculty of the University of Chicago. During the 1940–41 school year, Carnap was a visiting professor at Harvard University and was an active participant in a discussion group that included Bertrand Russell, Alfred Tarski, and W. V. O. Quine.

Soon after going to Chicago, Carnap joined with the sociologist Otto Neurath, a former fellow member of the Vienna Circle, and with an academic colleague, the Pragmatist philosopher Charles W. Morris, in founding the *International Encyclopedia of Unified Science*, which was published, beginning in 1938, as a series of monographs on general problems in the philosophy of science and on philosophical issues concerning mathematics or particular branches of empirical science.

Since his Vienna years, Carnap had been much concerned also with problems in logic and in the philosophy of language. He held that philosophical perplexities often arise from a misunderstanding or misuse of language and that the way to resolve them is by "logical analysis of language." On this point, he agreed with the "ordinary language" school of Analytic Philosophy, which had its origins in England. He differed from it, however, in insisting that more technical issues—e.g., those in the philosophy of science or of mathematics—cannot be adequately dealt with by considerations of ordinary linguistic usage but require clarification by reference to artificially constructed languages that are formulated in logical symbolism and that have their structure and interpretation precisely specified by so-called syntactic and semantic rules. Carnap developed these ideas and the theoretical apparatus for their implementation in a series of works, including *Logische Syntax der Sprache* (1934; *The Logical Syntax of Language*) and *Meaning and Necessity* (1947; 2nd enlarged ed., 1956).

Carnap's interest in artificial languages included advocacy of international auxiliary languages such as Esperanto and Interlingua to facilitate scholarly communication and to further international understanding.

One idea in logic and the theory of knowledge that occupied much of Carnap's attention was that of analyticity. In contrast to the 19th-century radical Empiricism of John Stuart Mill, Carnap and other Logical Empiricists held that the statements of logic and mathematics, unlike those of empirical science, are analytic—i.e., true solely by virtue of the meanings of their constituent terms—and that they can therefore be established a priori (without any empirical test). Carnap repeatedly returned to the task of formulating a precise characterization and theory of analyticity. His ideas were met with skepticism by some, however—among them Quine, who argued that the notion of analytic truth is inherently obscure and the attempt to delimit a class of statements that are true a priori should be abandoned as misguided.

From about 1945 onward, Carnap turned his efforts increasingly to problems of inductive reasoning and of rational belief and decision. His principal aim was to construct a formal system of inductive logic; its central concept, corresponding to that of deductive implication, would be that of probabilistic implication—or, more precisely, a concept representing the degree of rational credibility or of probability that a given body of evidence may be said to confer upon a proposed hypothesis. Carnap presented a rigorous theory of this kind in his *Logical Foundations of Probability* (1950).

Carnap spent the years from 1952 to 1954 at the Institute for Advanced Study in Princeton, where he continued his work in probability theory. Subsequently, he accepted a professorship at the University of California at Los Angeles. During those years and indeed until his death, Carnap was occupied principally with modifications and considerable extensions of his inductive logic.

SIR KARL POPPER

(b. July 28, 1902, Vienna, Austria—d. Sept. 17, 1994, Croydon, Greater London, Eng.)

Karl Popper was an Austrian-born British philosopher of natural and social science. He subscribed to an antideterminist metaphysics, believing that knowledge evolves from experience of the mind.

Although his first book, *Logik der Forschung* (1934; *The Logic of Scientific Discovery*), was published by the Vienna Circle of logical positivists, Popper rejected their inductive empiricism and developmental historicism. After studying mathematics, physics, and psychology at the University of Vienna, he taught philosophy at Canterbury University College, New Zealand (1937–45). In 1945 he became a reader in logic at the London School of Economics, and he served there as professor of logic and scientific method from 1949 until his retirement in 1969.

Popper's principal contribution to the philosophy of science rests on his rejection of the inductive method in the empirical sciences. According to this traditional view, a scientific hypothesis may be tested and verified by obtaining the repeated outcome of substantiating observations. As the Scottish empiricist David Hume had shown, however, only an infinite number of such confirming results could prove the theory correct. Popper argued instead that hypotheses are deductively validated by what he called the "falsifiability criterion." Under this method, a scientist seeks to discover an observed exception to his postulated rule. The absence of contradictory evidence thereby becomes corroboration of his theory. According to Popper, such pseudosciences as astrology, metaphysics, Marxist history, and Freudian psychoanalysis are not empirical sciences, because of their failure to adhere to the principle of falsifiability.

Popper's later works include *The Open Society and Its Enemies* (1945), *The Poverty of Historicism* (1957), and *Postscript to the Logic of Scientific Discovery*, 3 vol. (1981–82). He was knighted in 1965.

THEODOR WIESENGRUND ADORNO

(b. Sept. 11, 1903, Frankfurt am Main, Ger.—d. Aug. 6, 1969, Visp, Switz.)

Theodor Wiesengrund Adorno was a German philosopher who also wrote on sociology, psychology, and musicology. Adorno obtained a degree in philosophy from Johann Wolfgang Goethe University in Frankfurt in 1924. His early writings, which emphasize aesthetic development as important to historical evolution, reflect the influence of Walter Benjamin's application of Marxism to cultural criticism.

After teaching two years at the University of Frankfurt, Adorno immigrated to England in 1934 to escape the Nazi persecution of the Jews. He taught at the University of

Oxford for three years and then went to the United States (1938), where he worked at Princeton (1938–41) and then was codirector of the Research Project on Social Discrimination at the University of California, Berkeley (1941–48). Adorno and his colleague Max Horkheimer returned to the University of Frankfurt in 1949. There they rebuilt the Institute for Social Research and revived the Frankfurt school of critical theory, which contributed to the German intellectual revival after World War II.

One of Adorno's themes was civilization's tendency to self-destruction, as evinced by Fascism. In their widely influential book *Dialektik der Aufklärung* (1947; *Dialectic of Enlightenment*), Adorno and Horkheimer located this impulse in the concept of reason itself, which the Enlightenment and modern scientific thought had transformed into an irrational force that had come to dominate not only nature but humanity itself. The rationalization of human society had ultimately led to Fascism and other totalitarian regimes that represented a complete negation of human freedom. Adorno concluded that rationalism offers little hope for human emancipation, which might come instead from art and the prospects it offers for preserving individual autonomy and happiness. Adorno's other major publications are *Philosophie der neuen Musik* (1949; *Philosophy of Modern Music*), *The Authoritarian Personality* (1950, with others), *Negative Dialektik* (1966; *Negative Dialectics*), and *Ästhetische Theorie* (1970; "Aesthetic Theory").

JEAN-PAUL SARTRE

(b. June 21, 1905, Paris, France—d. April 15, 1980, Paris)

Jean-Paul Sartre was a French exponent of Existentialism—a philosophy acclaiming the freedom of the individual human being. Also a novelist and a playwright, he was awarded the Nobel Prize for Literature in 1964, but he declined it.

Early Life and Writings

Sartre lost his father at an early age and grew up in the home of his maternal grandfather, Carl Schweitzer, uncle of the medical missionary Albert Schweitzer and himself professor of German at the Sorbonne. The boy, who wandered in the Luxembourg Gardens of Paris in search of playmates, was small in stature and cross-eyed.

Sartre went to the Lycée Henri IV in Paris and, later on, after the remarriage of his mother, to the lycée in La Rochelle. From there he went to the prestigious École Normale Supérieure, from which he was graduated in 1929. Sartre resisted what he called "bourgeois marriage," but while still a student he formed with Simone de Beauvoir a union that remained a settled partnership in life. From 1931 until 1945 Sartre taught in the lycées of Le Havre, Laon, and, finally, Paris. Twice this career was interrupted, once by a year of study in Berlin and the second time when Sartre was drafted in 1939 to serve in World War II. He was made prisoner in 1940 and released a year later.

During his years of teaching in Le Havre, Sartre published *La Nausée* (1938; *Nausea*, 1949), his first claim to fame. This novel, written in the form of a diary, narrates the feeling of revulsion that a certain Roquentin undergoes when confronted with the world of matter—not merely the world of other people but the very awareness of his own body.

Sartre took over the phenomenological method, which proposes careful, unprejudiced description rather than deduction, from the German philosopher Edmund Husserl and used it with great skill in three successive publications: *L'Imagination* (1936; *Imagination: A Psychological Critique*, 1962), *Esquisse d'une théorie des émotions* (1939; *Sketch for a Theory of the Emotions*, 1962), and *L'Imaginaire: Psychologie phénoménologique de l'imagination* (1940; *The Psychology of Imagination*, 1950). But it was above all in *L'Être et le néant* (1943; *Being and Nothingness*, 1956) that Sartre revealed himself as a master of outstanding talent. Sartre places human consciousness, or no-thingness (*néant*), in opposition to being, or thingness (*être*). Consciousness is not-matter and by the same token escapes all determinism. The message, with all the implications it contains, is hopeful; yet the incessant reminder that human endeavor is and remains useless makes the book tragic as well.

Post-World War II Work

Having written his defense of individual freedom and human dignity, Sartre turned his attention to the concept of social responsibility. For many years he had shown great concern for the poor and the disinherited of all kinds. While a teacher, he had refused to wear a tie, as if he could shed his social class with his tie and thus come closer to the worker. Freedom itself, which at times in his previous writings appeared to be a gratuitous activity that needed no particular aim or purpose to be of value, became a tool for human struggle in his brochure *L'Existentialisme est un humanisme* (1946; *Existentialism and Humanism*, 1948). Freedom now implied social responsibility.

In his novels and plays Sartre began to bring his ethical message to the world at large. He started a four-volume novel in 1945 under the title *Les Chemins de la liberté*, of which three were eventually written: *L'Âge de raison* (1945; *The Age of Reason*, 1947), *Le Sursis* (1945; *The Reprieve*, 1947), and *La Mort dans l'âme* (1949; *Iron in the Soul*, 1950; U.S. title, *Troubled Sleep*, 1950).

After the publication of the third volume, Sartre changed his mind concerning the usefulness of the novel as a medium of communication and turned back to plays. All the plays, in their emphasis upon the raw hostility of man toward man, seem to be predominantly pessimistic; yet, according to Sartre's own confession, their content does not exclude the possibility of a morality of salvation. Other publications of the same period include a book, *Baudelaire* (1947), a vaguely ethical study on the French writer and poet Jean Genet entitled *Saint Genet, comédien et martyr* (1952; *Saint Genet, Actor and Martyr*, 1963), and innumerable articles that were published in *Les Temps Modernes*, the monthly review that Sartre and Simone de Beauvoir founded and edited.

Political Activities

After World War II, Sartre took an active interest in French political movements, and his leanings to the left became more pronounced. He became an outspoken admirer of the Soviet Union, although he did not become a member of the Communist Party. Upon the entry of Soviet tanks into Budapest in 1956, however, Sartre's hopes for communism were sadly crushed. He wrote in *Les Temps Modernes* a long article, "Le Fantôme de Staline," that condemned both the Soviet intervention and the submission of the French Communist Party to the dictates of Moscow. Over the years this critical attitude opened the way to a form of "Sartrian Socialism" that would find its expression in a new major work, *Critique de la raison dialectique* (1960; Eng. trans., of the introduction only, under the title *The Problem of Method*, 1963; U.S. title, *Search for a Method*).

Last Years

From 1960 until 1971 most of Sartre's attention went into the writing of a four-volume study called *Flaubert*. Two volumes with a total of some 2,130 pages appeared in the spring of 1971. This huge enterprise aimed at presenting the reader with a "total biography" of Gustave Flaubert, the famous French novelist, through the use of a double tool: on the one hand, Karl Marx's concept of history and class and, on the other, Sigmund Freud's illuminations of the dark recesses of the human soul through explorations into his childhood and family relations.

As if he himself were saturated by the prodigal abundance of his writings, Sartre moved away from his desk during 1971 and did very little writing. Under the motto that "commitment is an act, not a word," Sartre often went into the streets to participate in rioting, in the sale of left-wing literature, and in other activities that in his opinion were the way to promote "the revolution." Paradoxically enough, this same radical Socialist published in 1972 the third volume of the work on Flaubert, *L'Idiot de la famille*, another book of such density that only the bourgeois intellectual can read it.

The enormous productivity of Sartre came herewith to a close. Sartre became blind and his health deteriorated. In April 1980 he died of a lung tumor. His very impressive funeral, attended by some 25,000 people, was reminiscent of the burial of Victor Hugo, but without the official recognition that his illustrious predecessor had received.

Glossary

anti-Semitism: Hatred of Jewish people.

a priori: Related to what can be known through reason rather than observation.

causality: The assertion that there is a necessary connection among matters of fact.

dialectic: A technique of logical argument and analysis.

empiricism: The theory that experience is not only the best teacher, but the only true source of knowledge.

existentialism: A philosophy that stresses freedom of choice and responsibility for the consequences of one's actions.

fallacy: A wrong belief.

fascism: A political system headed by a dictator in which opposition is not permitted.

insoluble: Difficult to solve or explain.

kibbutz: A communal farm or settlement in Israel.

nihilism: The belief that morals have no value.

paradox: A statement that seems to contradict itself, but is essentially true.

phenomenology: The quest for the essences of things.

polemic: A controversy that attacks an existing opinion or doctrine.

posthumous: Occurring after the death of a person.

tautology: A statement that unnecessarily repeats a word or idea.

For More Information

BOOKS

Atkinson, Sam, Kelsie Besaw, and Pauline Savage. *What's the Point of Philosophy?* New York, NY: DK Publishing, 2022.

Gifford, Clive. *Philosophy for Everyone: Understand How Philosophers Have Helped Us to Tackle the Big Mysteries of Life*. London, England: Magic Cat Publishing, 2023.

Rachels, Stuart. *The Elements of Moral Philosophy*. New York, NY: McGraw Hill, 2023.

WEBSITES

Bertrand Russell Society
bertrandrussellsociety.org/read-russell/
The Bertrand Russell Society provides online links to works by Russell that are available in the public domain.

Crash Course Philosophy: Existentialism
thecrashcourse.com/courses/existentialism-crash-course-philosophy-16/
Learn about the philosophical school of thought called Existentialism and the contributions Jean-Paul Sartre made to its development.

Logic
kids.britannica.com/students/article/logic/275523
In this article from Britannica Kids, read about logic and how it's studied within the discipline of philosophy.

Index